Y0-AKF-076

```
J362.7          85-1177
Q8
Quiri
  Stranger Danger: A Safety Guide
for Children
```

DATE DUE			
OCT 3 1985	SEP 3 1987		
OCT 10 1985	SEP 2 4 1987		
NOV 2 8 1985	AUG 3 1999		
FEB 1 3 1986	APR 4		
MAR 6 1986	MAY 3 0		
APR 3 1986	FEB - 6 1992		
April 24, 1986			
MAY 1 5 1986			
JUL 3 1986			
AUG 7 1986			
AUG 2 8 1986			
SEP 1 1 1986			

Chanute Public Library
Chanute, Kansas 66720

STRANGER DANGER

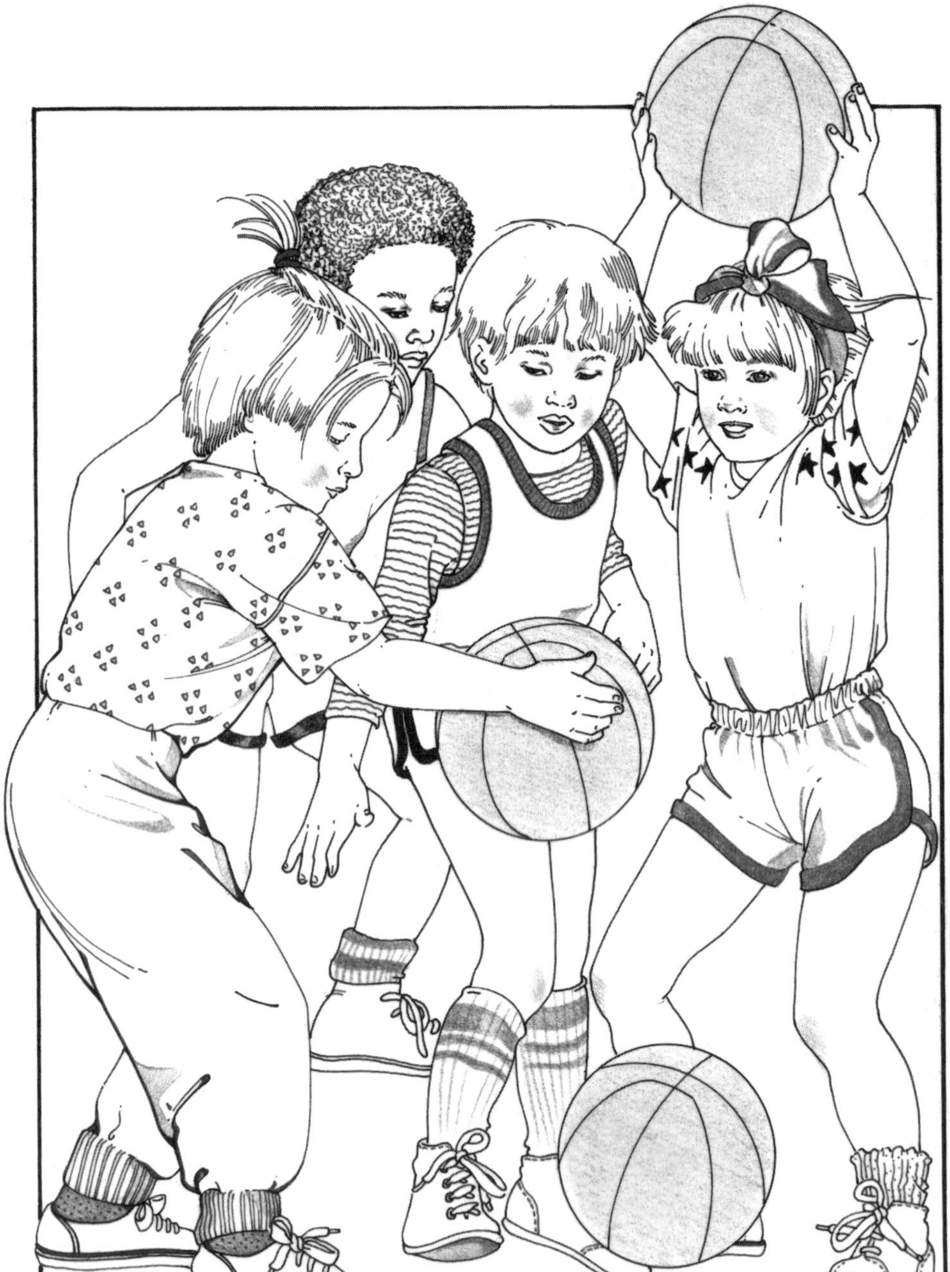

STRANGER DANGER

by Patricia Ryon Quiri
and Suzanne I. Powell

illustrated by Marika Hahn

Julian Messner   New York

Copyright © 1985 by Patricia Ryon Quiri
and Suzanne I. Powell

All rights reserved
including the right of reproduction
in whole or in part in any form.
Published by Julian Messner,
A Division of Simon & Schuster, Inc.
Simon & Schuster Building
Rockefeller Center
1230 Avenue of the Americas
New York, New York 10020

JULIAN MESSNER and colophon are
trademarks of Simon & Schuster, Inc.

Manufactured in the United States of America

Design by Meri Shardin

Library of Congress Cataloguing in Publication Data
Quiri, Patricia.
　Stranger danger.

　Bibliography: p.
　Includes index.
　　1. Children and strangers—Juvenile literature.
2. Child abuse—Prevention—Juvenile literature.
3. Child molesting—Prevention—Juvenile literature.
I. Powell, Suzanne. II. Title.
HQ784.S8Q57　1985　　　362.7′044　　　85-2945
ISBN: 0-671-55044-6

*To our sons Robbie, Bradford, Ben and Eric.
Be happy, be safe. We love you.*

Can you name a stranger you know? Of course you can't. A stranger is someone you have never seen before. A stranger is someone whose name you do not know.

Strangers come in all shapes and sizes. You may see strangers in stores, in parks, in a church or a synagogue, even in your own neighborhood. You will see them almost everywhere you go. Some people may smile at you and say "Hi" just to be friendly. Others may be friendly just to gain your trust. Because you can't tell the dangerous strangers from the friendly ones, you must be very careful with everyone you do not know.

You may have heard of children who had been taken away—kidnapped. Some of these children were hurt. Others have never returned to their homes.

This book can help protect you from danger. It gives many hints and tips to keep you safe from strangers who mean to harm you. You'll read about how children just like you may be approached by a stranger or touched in a way that makes them feel bad or uncomfortable. Think about what you would do in each situation, then read about the best way to protect yourself. You *can* be safe if you remember to do what is suggested below.

Strangers are everywhere. Most of them mean you no harm, but there are some who may want to take you away from your parents and friends. To do this, they may try to trick you into coming with them. In the following story, Amy learns that one way strangers try to fool you is by pretending to know you or your parents.

A stranger may call you by name. He may tell you that your mother or father sent him to you. He may tell you that your mother or father is hurt. What would you do in a situation like this?

Find out what happens to Amy:

Amy put the phone down. She was excited. She called to her mother. "Mom, Linda wants to know if I can come to her house to play and have lunch. May I, please?"

"Yes, you may," answered her mother.

"Yippee!" Amy shouted. She and Linda were best friends.

"Now remember," her mother warned. "Stay on the sidewalk and call me as soon as you get to Linda's. And please, remember never to talk to strangers."

"I won't, Mom. And I promise to call." She kissed her mother and went out the door.

Amy was only two streets away from her friend's house when a car pulled over to the curb a few feet from her. The driver was a middle-aged man. A woman seated next to him rolled down the window and called out, "Amy, your mother asked us to pick you up. She's had an accident. Come with us and we'll take you to her."

Amy paused. If her mother really was hurt, she should go with them. But she didn't know these people. She remembered that her mother had told her to stay on the sidewalk and never to speak to strangers. What do YOU think Amy should do?

Amy became frightened. She quickly turned and ran the rest of the way to her friend's house. After telling Linda's mother what had happened, she called home. Her mother answered the phone and told Amy that everything was fine. She said that Amy had done the right thing by running from the strangers. Is this what YOU would have done?

Here are some safety tips to remember when you are all alone on the street:

1. Always tell Mom or Dad where you're going.
2. Never talk to people you do not know. Don't get close to a stranger's car. No matter what a stranger may tell you, even if he or she pretends to know you, don't go anywhere alone with him or her.
3. Whenever possible, walk with a friend or a grownup.
4. Call home when you have arrived and let Mom or Dad know you are safe.
5. Always walk facing automobile traffic, not in the same direction as the traffic.
6. If possible, remember the license plate number of any stranger who approaches you. Report this to the police.

It's always fun to make a new friend. It makes you feel good when someone new likes you and thinks you are special. But you must be very careful when getting to know someone new, especially if this stranger is much older than you are.

What would you do if a person you did not know tried to make friends with you and take you somewhere with him? This happens to Jason one Saturday afternoon. Find out what he did:

Jason and his friends would meet each Saturday morning at their neighborhood park for a fast-paced, fun game of football.

Many people passing by would stop to watch the boys, some for a long time.

As Jason and his friends played their game one day, a man watched from a nearby bench. When the boys took a break, he walked over to them, a smile on his face.

"Hi, boys!" said the man enthusiastically. "You've got a great game going."

"Yeah, thanks," responded a couple of the boys.

"I used to play football in high school and college," the man continued. "I started out playing with my friends, just like you're doing."

"Do you have any plays you could show us?" one of Jason's friends asked.

"Sure," said the man. "Would you like to see some?"

"Yeah!" shouted the boys.

The man joined in, first showing them some new plays, and then becoming part of the game.

After they had played for an hour together, Jason noticed the time and announced, "I have to go. I promised my mom I'd be home for lunch."

"I'll give you a ride home, Jason," offered the man. "My car is parked right over there. I ought to get going myself."

A ride back sounded good to Jason, but even though this man had played ball with Jason and his friends, and seemed friendly, Jason did not really know him. What do YOU think Jason should do?

Jason said, "No, thank you." He straddled his bicycle and rode quickly home. He told his parents what had happened. They told him that he had made a wise decision to go straight home by himself. Is this what YOU would have done?

Here are a few things to remember if a stranger approaches you when you're playing with a group of friends:

1. Even though a stranger might join your game and be very friendly, he still remains a stranger.
2. Never tell a stranger where you live.
3. Never accept a ride from a stranger.
4. Remind your friends never to go anywhere with a stranger.

Your own home is a safe place. When you're at home alone, however, you must be extra careful with strangers who telephone or come to the door. A stranger should never know when you're all alone.

Sarah is taking care of her little brother while her parents are out to dinner. Someone she does not know telephones. What would you do if you were in Sarah's situation?

Here's what Sarah does:

"What's wrong, Mom?" questioned Sarah as she bounded into the kitchen.

"Oh, your father and I were planning on going out to dinner tonight," sighed Mrs. Johnson. "But it seems all of our sitters have other plans. No one can sit with you and your brother."

"That's an easy problem to solve." Sarah smiled. "I'm twelve years old. You said that when I was twelve, I could stay home alone with Matthew."

"I don't know, Sarah," responded Mrs. Johnson uneasily. After thinking for a few minutes, she brightened. "We won't be out very late. Let's give it a try."

As the Johnsons were leaving that evening, Mrs. Johnson gave Sarah last-minute instructions. "Remember, keep the doors locked and don't open them to anyone you don't know. If anyone you don't know telephones, simply take a message and tell the caller that I'll return their call in a few minutes. Is that clear?"

"Yes, Mom. Don't worry. We'll be fine." Sarah responded. "Now go and have a good time."

"Okay. We'll be home early," said Mrs. Johnson.

Later that evening, the telephone rang while Sarah and Matthew were watching television. Sarah jumped up and answered it. "Hello," she said.

"Hello," said a man. "Is your father home?"

"No," replied Sarah.

"Is your mother home?" asked the man whose voice she did not recognize.

"No," said Sarah, forgetting her mother's careful instructions. "They're out to dinner."

"Are they going to be out late?" the man asked.

"Not too late," Sarah answered. "May I ask who's calling?"

"Are you all alone?" asked the man, ignoring her question.

"Who are you?" asked Sarah, beginning to feel uncomfortable.

The man did not answer. A few seconds later, Sarah heard him hang up.

Sarah stared at the phone. She didn't like what had just happened. It frightened her that the caller had hung up so abruptly. And his questions had upset her, also. Sarah did not know the man who had called. What do YOU think Sarah should do?

Sarah called Mrs. Brown, her next-door neighbor. She explained what had happened, and told

Mrs. Brown that she was frightened. Mrs. Brown came to stay with Sarah and Matthew. When the Johnsons returned, Sarah told them about the telephone call. Mr. and Mrs. Johnson explained that the instructions they had given her before they left were extremely important. She should *not* have told the man that her parents were not at home. She should have simply told him that her parents were busy and that they would call him back as soon as they had a chance. Sarah's parents told her that she *did* show good judgment by calling Mrs. Brown, but that she should take stronger precautions when home alone.

Here are a few important safety tips for you to remember when you're at home alone:

1. Do not let an unfamiliar person know you are alone.
2. Never answer the door without first making sure you know who it is. If the caller persists in ringing the bell or knocking, telephone a neighbor or the police for help.
3. Do not tell a stranger where your parents are. Tell the caller that they are not available to talk at the moment, but will call back if he or she would leave a message.
4. If an unfamiliar caller continues to ask unnecessary questions or threatens you in any way, hang up immediately and call someone to help you.
5. Always have the telephone number of the place where your parents will be.
6. Make sure you have a list of emergency telephone numbers, such as the police, fire department, and neighbors.

New experiences—like a job, a ride on a motorcycle, or a trip to the zoo—are exciting, and meeting new people can be fun. But if a stranger asks you to go with him anywhere without telling your parents first, you must be very careful.

If a stranger seemed very kind and offered you an interesting opportunity, what would you do? In this story, John is in that situation. See what he does:

The familiar buzzing sounds rang in John's ears as he entered the video arcade. He looked forward to spending some time there while his mother went shopping in the mall. After John's tenth birthday, his parents felt he could handle himself responsibly while his mother shopped.

John searched around for his favorite video game and quickly spotted one that was available. He played several games, concentrating so hard that he did not notice a young man and woman approach him.

"Hi!" said the man, as the twosome suddenly appeared behind John.

"What's your name?" asked the woman.

John did not answer. He felt rather annoyed that they were bothering him.

"It's okay. You don't have to tell us your name," continued the woman. "We were just admiring how well you play the game."

John gave them a half-smile and continued his game.

"I think he might be perfect for the part in the commercial we're trying to cast," said the man to the woman.

"Hey, I think you might be right," the woman exclaimed.

Their remarks caught John's attention. "What are you talking about?"

"We work for a production company here in town that produces commercials for various products," the man explained. "We're now working on a commercial about video equipment and we need several kids your age to play the video games on the commercial. You'd be perfect for the part. Would you like to give it a try?"

"Well ... I don't know," answered John hesitantly. "What would I have to do?"

"We can take you to the studio right now for an audition," said the woman. "Our van is parked outside."

"You will even be paid for being in the commercial," added the woman.

"I'd better go and find my mother and ask her first," said John.

"Oh, why do that?" said the man quickly. "We want this to be a surprise for her and the rest of your family."

"But she'll be here in a few minutes looking for me. She'll be worried if I'm not here." John explained.

"It won't take that long. We can bring you right back. Just think how excited your mother will be when she finds out you're going to be in a TV commercial," the woman said, her eyes sparkling with excitement.

John was feeling so many different things.

17

This commercial sounded pretty neat. And these people had actually picked HIM to do it! Even though the man and woman seemed very nice, however, John did not know who they were. He did not recognize them. What do YOU think John should do?

John insisted on finding his mother first. He knew that he must ask permission before leaving the mall with anyone else.

After John found his mother, he explained to her what had taken place. The two went back to the arcade, but the couple who had approached John were gone. John's mother explained to him that strangers sometimes entice kids by promising them exciting things or money to get them away. John did the right thing by finding his mother first. Is this what YOU would have done?

Here are some things to remember if you are approached by a stranger who offers you a job, or something else that sounds exciting:

1. Always insist on getting permission from your parents first. Anyone who is in business legally and who means you no harm will want and need their permission.
2. Be suspicious of people who ask you to do something secretly, or as a "surprise" for your family.
3. Don't be fooled into accepting an exciting offer without consulting your parents first.

A hug and a kiss from people who love you, like your mom and dad, make you feel good. A pat on the head from your big brother or holding hands with your best friend shows friendship and warmth. But there are times when the way a person touches you makes you feel uncomfortable. No matter who the person is, you have the right to tell him or her to stop touching if it makes you feel bad.

Joanie's babysitter touches her in a way Joanie doesn't like. Find out what Joanie decides to do:

Joanie peeked shyly around the staircase. Her mother was giving the new sitter last-minute instructions before going out for the evening with her husband.

"Oh, there you are, Joanie!" exclaimed Mrs. Carpenter. "Come meet Laura. She's going to take care of you tonight." Mrs. Carpenter turned to Laura and said, "I'm so glad to find you. It's not easy to find sitters when you're new in town. I hope you and Joanie get along okay. She loves to read and do puzzles. And she enjoys playing games. If you have any problems or questions, here is the number at which you can reach us."

Joanie walked into the kitchen after her parents had gone.

"Hi, Joanie," said Laura with a smile.

"Hi," returned Joanie timidly.

"How old are you? I bet you're around seven."

Joanie's face brightened. Her smile revealed two large dimples and a space in her mouth where she had recently lost a tooth.

"I'm only six. But everyone thinks I'm a lot older," responded Joanie.

The evening passed quickly. Joanie and Laura read together and played a few board games. After they finished a quick snack, Laura glanced at her watch and said, "Okay, Joanie. It's time for your bath."

"Oh," groaned Joanie. "Can't we play one more game?"

"We'll see if we have time after your bath. Come on. Upstairs you go!" responded Laura.

While Laura ran the bath water, Joanie undressed. When she was in the tub, Laura reached for the soap.

"Time to soap you up," said Laura.

"Oh, I always wash myself," replied Joanie.

"I'll do it tonight, Joanie. After all, I'm your sitter and your mother did tell you to mind me."

After a while, Joanie began to feel uncomfortable.

"Laura, I'm all clean now. Why are you still putting soap all over me?" questioned Joanie, squirming beneath Laura's hand.

"Okay, you can get out now. But don't get dressed yet. I know a fun game we can play. Go into your room and dry off. Then lie down on your bed. I'll clean up the bathroom."

Joanie went into her room with a towel wrapped around her. She dried herself and sat down on the bed. Laura walked in a few minutes later.

"Lie down on your bed, Joanie," said Laura as she reached to take the towel off Joanie. "We're going to play a game, but you must promise not to tell your parents about it. It will be our secret."

"But why can't I get dressed?" cried Joanie. "I'm cold!" She reached for her pajamas.

"Because one of the rules of the game is that you can't have any clothes on. Give me your pajamas." She grabbed Joanie's clothes and threw them aside. "I'll tell you what. I'll bring you a new puzzle the next time I come over if you'll play this secret game." Laura pushed Joanie down on the bed and started to touch her. Joanie suddenly became afraid. Laura had seemed so nice earlier, but now she was making Joanie feel uncomfortable and frightened. She didn't think Laura should be touching her like this. What do YOU think Joanie should do?

Joanie quickly rolled off the bed and screamed, "Stop touching me!" as loudly as she could. She grabbed her pajamas and raced into her parents' bedroom and called her parents, who came home right away, and sent the sitter home.

When Joanie told her parents what had happened, they gave her a big hug and told her she did just the right thing. Laura was sick to touch her like that and needed help. Joanie would never have to see her again. Joanie was glad she told her parents. Is that what YOU would have done?

Here are some things to remember if a sitter, or anyone else, should ever try to touch you in a place that makes you feel uncomfortable:

1. Everyone has private parts of his or her body. No one should ask to see or touch these parts, except your doctor.
2. If someone touches you where you feel they shouldn't, scream and run away. Tell your mom or dad exactly what happened.

3. It's okay to question whatever a sitter, teacher, or anyone else does while your parents are not around.
4. Don't be fooled by someone who offers you a special treat, or tells you to keep anything a "secret."

Collecting for a school project or for charity usually means going from house to house and requesting money from the people who live there. It can be lots of fun, you'll meet interesting people, and you'll be working for a good cause.

But there are special safety rules to follow when you go door-to-door. In the next story, Bill and Randy meet a friendly person who invites them inside his home while he looks for his wallet. What would you do if this happened to you? This is what Bill and Randy did:

The school bell rang loudly. Another school day had finally ended.

"Please remain in your seats, class. I must finish handing out the carnival tickets and selling sheets," announced Mrs. Lockhart above the chattering of her class. "I'd like all of you to sell as many tickets as you can," she continued. "Remember that the money will be used to buy new playground equipment. Those who sell the most tickets will be treated to a special pizza party after the carnival!"

The boys and girls clapped and cheered loudly.

"Okay. Everyone has his tickets. Please remember to be with someone else when you go up to each door. Be *very* careful," warned Mrs. Lockhart.

Bill and Randy headed for their lockers, eager to get home and change their clothes. They wanted to be the first ones out in the neighborhood to sell their carnival tickets.

"I'll meet you as soon as I change," said Randy.

"Don't forget the envelope for the money!" yelled Bill, as Randy raced down the street.

The boys met a few minutes later, ready to begin their door-to-door visits.

After covering their neighbors' houses, they found they had only a few more tickets left to sell.

"Let's try some new streets," said Randy. "We don't have to be home for another hour or so."

"Great! Let's go!" exclaimed Bill, heading for the corner.

Soon they stood on the steps of a two-story brick home waiting patiently for someone to answer their knock. It had begun to rain, so Randy and Bill pulled up the hoods of their jackets.

"Hello, boys," said a tall, middle-aged man as he looked out the door. "What can I do for you?"

"Hi. We're selling tickets to our school carnival," explained Randy. "Would you like to buy some?

"How much are they?" inquired the stranger.

"They're 25¢ each, or five for a dollar," Bill replied, a hopeful smile on his face.

"Let me check my wallet and see if I can help you out," said the man. He left Bill and Randy waiting anxiously at the door. A few minutes later the man returned.

"It seems that I have misplaced my wallet," said the man. "I know it's in here somewhere. Why don't you come inside out of the rain while I look around for it?"

Bill and Randy looked at each other. They wanted to sell the rest of their tickets. They also wanted to get out of the rain. But neither of them knew this man. What do YOU think Bill and Randy did?

Bill and Randy told the man that they would wait outside. The man said okay, and went back to look for his wallet. He found it and bought some carnival tickets from the boys. Later, when Bill told his mother what happened, she told him that he and Bill were right not go to into a stranger's house. Is this what YOU would have done?

Here are some safety tips to remember when you approach strangers at their homes:

1. Never go into a stranger's house.
2. Stand far enough away from the person, so he or she cannot touch you.
3. Always do your selling or collecting before dark.
4. When going door-to-door, always use the buddy system. It's more fun, and much safer than going alone!

Most of the people you see every day are good people who want you to be safe and happy. Most of your teachers, policemen and others in your neighborhood care about you. But some people, even those you think you should trust, can hurt you if you aren't careful.

What would you do if a teacher touched you in a way that made you feel bad? Becky had been taking piano lessons from Mr. Webster for almost a year. He seemed very nice, and his wife baked delicious cookies for Becky to eat after her lesson. But this day, Mrs. Webster isn't there and Mr. Webster is acting different. He starts to touch Becky in a way that makes her uncomfortable. Let's see how Becky handles the situation:

Ten-year-old Becky dashed into the kitchen, her thick braids bouncing on her back. She was ready for another lesson from Mr. Webster, her music teacher. Her mother was taking her to his home, where the lessons were always given.

Mrs. Brown and her daughter left the house and walked up the street. As they neared the Webster house, Mrs. Brown said, "While you're having your lesson, I'm going to run across the street to Aunt Peggy's for a visit. See you later, dear."

Becky stood on the Websters' front porch and rang the doorbell. Mr. Webster greeted her. "Come in Becky," he said warmly. "We've got a lot of work to do before your recital. Hang your coat in the closet and come sit down."

"Where's Mrs. Webster today? I don't smell any of her homemade chocolate fudge cookies," smiled Becky.

"Oh, she decided to run some errands this afternoon," replied Mr. Webster. "She'll probably be back before the end of your lesson."

Becky sat down in front of the shiny black piano and began her warm-up exercises. Mr. Webster took a seat next to her.

"Ah, your fingers seem to be in good form today, Becky. Do two more scales and we'll start on this piece," he said as he pointed to some sheets of music.

The first half of her lesson flew by. Becky stood up to stretch.

"Tired?" asked Mr. Webster. "This is where my back hurts sometimes after playing for awhile." He started to rub Becky's back gently.

"Oh, it's fine now," replied Becky, as she took her seat once again.

"Your braids are so long and pretty," said Mr. Webster softly. He reached out and touched Becky's hair. His hand continued down her back. She squirmed beneath his touch.

"It's all right, Becky," whispered Mr. Webster. "I'm just admiring how pretty you've become."

He shifted his position and flipped through her music. "Let's change some of this. These lines should be played slower. Take these over to the couch," he said as he handed her the music. "I'll get a pencil."

Becky took the sheets to the couch and sat down. She thought Mr. Webster was acting kind of strange.

He came back into the room and sat down beside her. He reached for the music and began making some changes.

"Well, I think that will work, Becky," commented Mr. Webster. "I think you'll notice a big difference." He patted her leg and kept his hand there. "You know, you remind me of my daughter when she was your age," he continued, rubbing her leg.

Becky started to stand up.

"It's all right, Becky. I won't hurt you. Sit down." He pulled her down and put his arm around her.

Becky began to feel uncomfortable. She wished Mrs. Webster would get home. She couldn't understand why Mr. Webster kept touching her, but she knew it didn't feel right. She didn't like this at all. What do YOU think Becky should do?

Becky dashed from the couch to the closet where her coat was hung. She turned to her instructor and said in a quivering voice, "I don't like you to touch me like that, Mr. Webster. Don't you ever do that again." She slammed the door and ran across the street to her Aunt Peggy's house, where she sobbingly told her mother what had happened. Is this what YOU would have done?

Here are some safety tips to remember should any stranger—or even someone you know—try to touch you in a way that upsets you:

1. Get away from the person if you can. Yell, if necessary.
2. No one should touch you in any way that makes you feel bad or uncomfortable.
3. Tell your mom or dad about anyone who may do that to you.

In all the situations you have read about in this book, the children used pretty good judgment. They walked or ran from the person and the situation and found help. They knew that they could, and should, tell their parents about anything bad that happens to them. There are people who are sick and try to hurt you, and there are laws to protect you from them. By telling your parents about a stranger who bothers you, you could be saving another child from the same danger.

Remember the rules of *safety* when dealing with a stranger who approaches you or with anyone who makes you feel uncomfortable by touching you:

1. Never go anywhere with strangers.
2. Stand a safe distance from a stranger or a stranger's car.
3. Never accept candy, toys, rides or jobs from strangers without getting permission from your parents first. These offers may be a way of tricking you.

4. Never walk alone, especially after dark.
5. Never tell a stranger where you live.
6. Never let a stranger into your house, *especially* if your parents are not at home.
7. Do not be alarmed or frightened by a stranger who tells you something is wrong with your mom or dad. Find someone you know or a policeman to help you.
8. Don't let a stranger trick you by threatening to hurt or harm you.
9. Always tell Mom or Dad where you are going.
10. If a stranger ever touches you or grabs you, scream as loudly as you can. Try to get away and run for help.
11. Remember that there are good touches and bad touches. Good touches are kisses and hugs from people you love and who care about you. Bad touches are touches in places that make you feel uncomfortable or bad.
12. You have a right to body privacy. No one should ask to see or touch your private parts.
13. You have a right to protect yourself by screaming, running away and reporting whatever took place to someone you trust.

Unfortunately, many children have never learned their safety rules. When approached by a stranger or when in an uncomfortable situation, they did not know how to respond to the danger and stay safe. These children have often been taken away from their parents by strangers. Some of them have been found and safely returned home, but others are still missing or have been harmed. Try not to let this happen to YOU.

Remember . . . you're a very special person to those who love you.

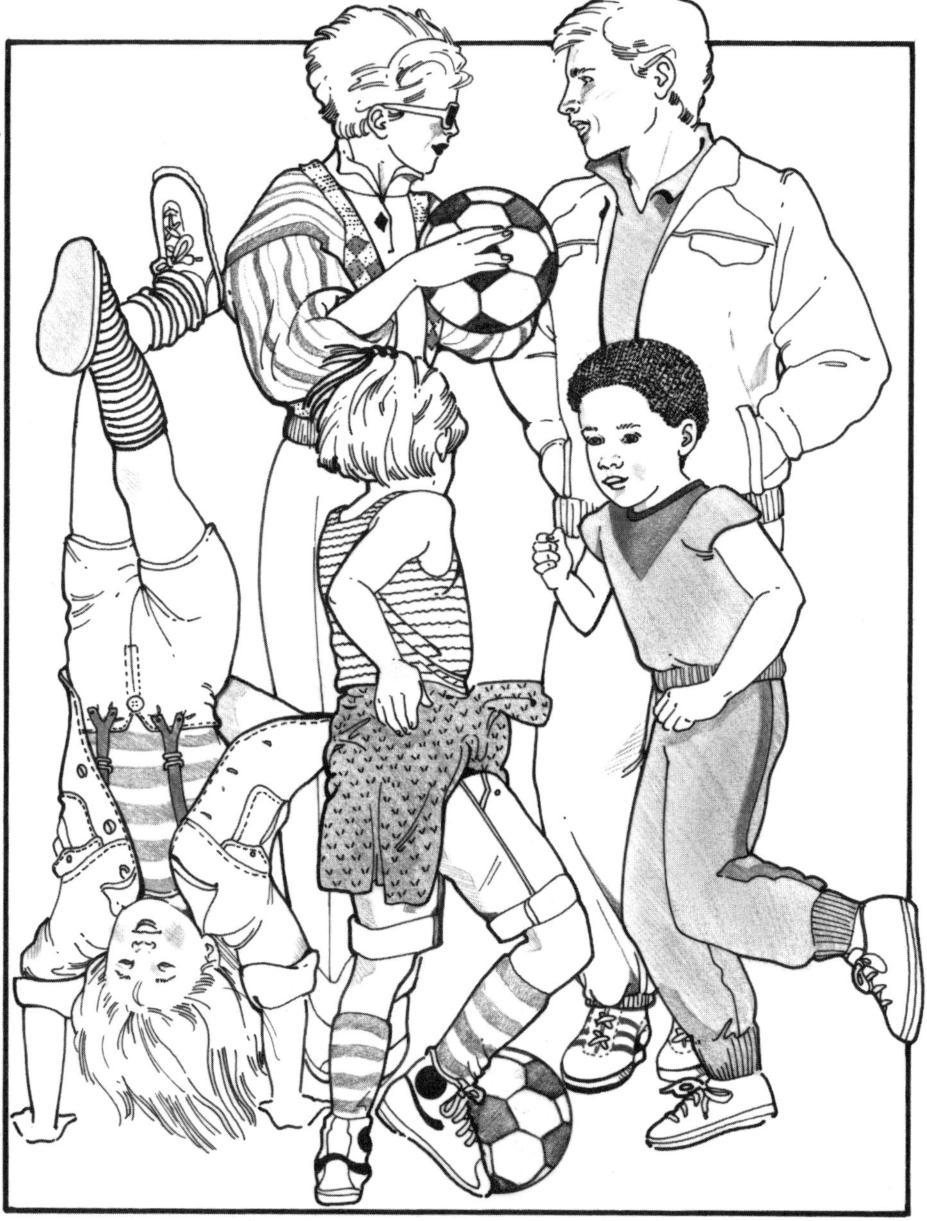

For further reading on this subject, here is a list of related books which might be of interest to you:

1. *Jenny's New Game*: A Guide For Parents to Protect your Children against Kidnapping by Laurella Brough Cross.
2. *No More Secrets For Me* by Oralee Wachter. A book for children about sexual abuse.
3. *Strangers* by Dorothy Chlad. A book for pre-schoolers concerning children and strangers.
4. *Red Light Green Light*. A coloring book for children about sexual abuse.

If you need help or know someone who does, here are some nationwide organizations which might be of help to you:

1. National Chapter for Prevention of Child Abuse
   P.O. Box 2866
   Chicago, Ill. 60690
2. Child Find Missing Children—New York
   (800) 431-5005
3. Missing Children Help Center—Tampa, Fla.
   (800) 872-5437
4. Missing Children Hotline—Washington, D.C.
   (800) 843-5678

5. The Adam Walsh Resource Center
   1876 North University Drive Suite 306
   Fort Lauderdale, Florida   33322
   (305) 475-4847

About the Authors

Patricia Ryon Quiri lives in Grand Rapids, Michigan. She is an elementary school teacher with an elementary education degree from Alfred University in New York state. She was born on Long Island.

Suzanne I. Powell lives in Grand Rapids, Michigan. She is an elementary school teacher with an elementary education degree from Central Michigan University. She also has a Master's degree from Michigan State University. She was born in Montgomery, Alabama.

Both authors are parents.